HOUGHTON MIFFLIN

Reading

A Legacy of Literacy

Let's Be Friends

Senior Authors
J. David Cooper
John J. Pikulski

Authors
Patricia A. Ackerman
Kathryn H. Au
David J. Chard
Gilbert G. Garcia
Claude N. Goldenberg
Marjorie Y. Lipson
Susan E. Page
Shane Templeton
Sheila W. Valencia
MaryEllen Vogt

Consultants
Linda H. Butler
Linnea C. Ehri
Carla B. Ford

HOUGHTON MIFFLIN   BOSTON • MORRIS PLAINS, NJ

California • Colorado • Georgia • Illinois • New Jersey • Texas

Cover and title page photography by Michelle Joyce.

Cover illustration by Anna Rich.

Acknowledgments begin on page 156.

Printed in the U.S.A.

ISBN: 0-618-15669-0

456789-DW-06 05 04 03 02 01

Let's Look Around! 12

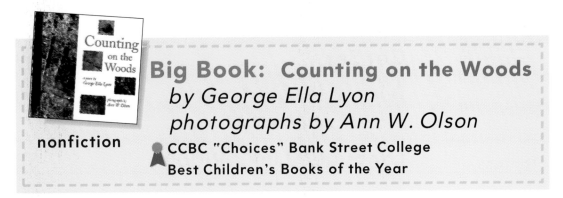

nonfiction

Big Book: Counting on the Woods
by George Ella Lyon
photographs by Ann W. Olson
CCBC "Choices" Bank Street College
Best Children's Books of the Year

nonfiction

Phonics Library:
Cabs, Cabs, Cabs
Fall Naps
Pam Can Pack

Big Book: Pearl's First Prize Plant
by A. Delaney

fiction

fantasy

Phonics Library:
Lots of Picking
Bill Bird
Tim's Cat

Big Book: Hilda Hen's Scary Night
by Mary Wormell

fantasy

Bank Street College Best Children's
Books of the Year

nonfiction

Phonics Library:
Let's Trim the Track!
Brad's Quick Rag Tricks
Fran Pig's Brick Hut

Additional Resources

On My Way Practice Reader

Mack
by James M. Pare

Apple Picking
by Irma Singer

The Crab
by Alice E. Lisson

Theme Paperbacks

Barnyard Tracks
by Dee Dee Duffy
illustrated by Janet Marshall

Mud!
by Charnan Simon
photographs by
Dorothy Handelman

When Tiny Was Tiny
by Cari Meister
illustrated by Rich Davis

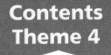

Family and Friends 84

realistic
fiction

Big Book: The Secret Code
by Dana Meachen Rau
illustrated by Bari Weissman

realistic
fiction

Phonics Library:
Knock, Knock
Miss Nell
Deb and Bess

Big Book: Caribbean Dream
by Rachel Isadora
🎗 Americas Award Commended List

realistic
fiction

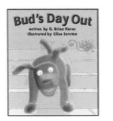

realistic
fiction

Phonics Library:
Buzzing Bug
Duff in the Mud
Jess and Mom

Additional Resources

On My Way Practice Reader

Family Day
by Naomi Parker

Best Friends
by Ann Takman

The Bug Jug Band
by Dan McDaniel

Theme Paperbacks

Biscuit Finds a Friend
by Alyssa Satin Capucilli
illustrated by Pat Schories

Come! Sit! Speak!
by Charnan Simon
illustrated by Bari Weissman

The Day the Sheep Showed Up
by David McPhail

To read about more good books, go to Education Place.

www.eduplace.com/kids

This Internet reading incentive program provides thousands of titles for children to read.

www.bookadventure.org

Let's Look Around!

Read Together

Sleeping Outdoors

Under the dark
    is a star,

Under the star
    is a tree,

Under the tree
    is a blanket,

And under the
    blanket is me.

by Marchette Chute

Seasons

Seasons

written by Michael Medearis

Words to Know

animal	see
bird	fat
cold	nap
fall	cap
flower	sacks
full	pack
look	bugs
of	

It is fall.

Jack can get a cap.

It can get cold.

Jack can get a flower.
Jack can see a bird. Tap, tap, tap!
It can get big, fat bugs.

Look! The fat animal can nap.
Dad and Jack pack sacks full
of nuts.

Michael Medearis

16

Seasons

written by Michael Medearis

Fall

Fall is here.
It can get cool.

Lots of leaves fit in a sack.
I will pack ten sacks full of leaves.

Birds go south in the fall.
Animals get fat for the winter.

Winter

Winter is here!
It can get cold.
Does it get cold where you live?

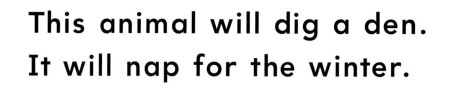

This animal will dig a den.
It will nap for the winter.

Snow can fall in the winter.
Snow can be lots of fun!

Look at my big snowman!
I add bits of coal and a carrot.

Look! My snowman has a little cap.

Spring

Spring is here!
It can get wet in the spring.
I will not get wet!

Tap, tap, tap!
A bird can tap and get bugs.
I can tap and see the sap.

Here is a spring flower.
I will see lots of flowers in the spring.

Summer

Summer is here.
It can get hot.
We jump in to get cool.

It is not hot here!
I am wet and cool.

It is hot, but I have a fan.
I will get cool with my fan.

I pack my red box and get my
big, big net.

Pull! Pull!

Quick! Get the net!

Dad and I got a big bass!

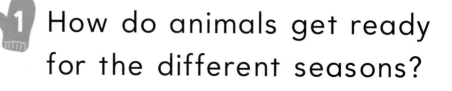
Think About the Story

Seasons

written by Michael Medearis

 1 How do animals get ready for the different seasons?

 2 What different things do people do in different seasons? Why?

3 What happens during the seasons where you live?

Write a Sentence

Write a sentence about your favorite season.

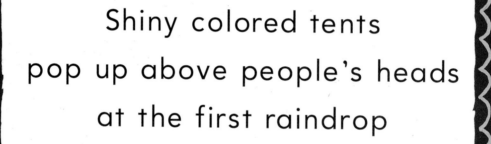

Shiny colored tents
pop up above people's heads
at the first raindrop

by Myra Cohn Livingston

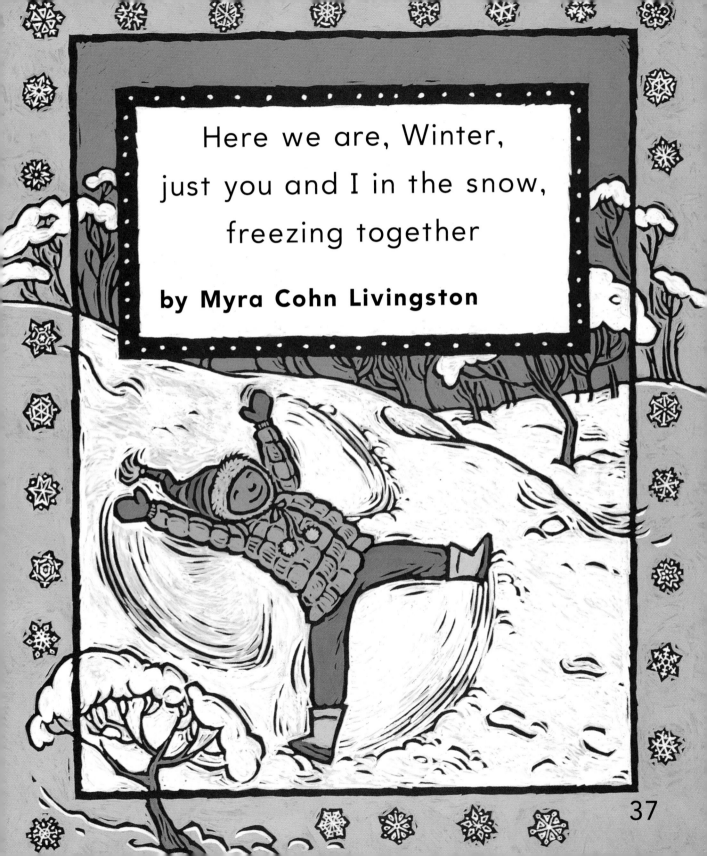

Here we are, Winter,
just you and I in the snow,
freezing together

by **Myra Cohn Livingston**

Words to Know

all	first	bib
call	never	in
why	will	lips
paper	miss	digs
eat	Pig	licked
every	big	picked
shall	six	backing

The ad in the paper said,
"Eat all you can at Big C's."

"I will call Pig," said Fox.

"Pig, why not eat at Big C's?" said Fox.
"I never miss big, big eats," said Pig.
"Shall we get to Big C's at six, Fox?"

Pig picked up every bib he had.
"Who digs in first, Fox?" said Pig.
Pig licked his big lips.
"Not I, Pig," said Fox, backing away.

Meet the Author and Illustrator
Francisco Mora

Mr. C's Dinner

written and illustrated
by Francisco Mora

Hen got a paper.
Hen sat to read the paper.

Fox got a paper.
Fox looked at his paper.

Pig got a paper.
The paper has a map on it!

The map tells where to go.

"We shall not miss it at six," Hen said.
"Who is Mr. C?" said Pig.

They all met at Mr. C's den at six.
A big sign said, "Mr. C's Den."
"Let's go in," said Fox.

Every animal got a big bib.
"We all have bibs," said Pig.
"Where is Mr. C?" said Hen.

Fox licked his lips.
Pig picked a big dish.
"Where is Mr. C?" said Pig.

"Fox, call Mr. C," said Hen.
Fox called, "Mr. C, we are here!"

Tap, tap, tap. Mr. C is here.
Mr. C looked in at the animals.
The animals looked at Mr. C.

"Mr. C is Coyote!" they all yelled.
"Will you eat me?" said Pig,
backing away.

"Never!" said Mr. C.
"I will not eat you."

"My dinner is not a big,
bad trick," said Mr. C.
"Let's eat! Who digs in first?"

"I will dig in first!" said Hen. "Why not?"
They all had Mr. C's yams for dinner.

Think About the Story

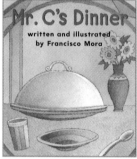

 Why did Mr. C send the invitation?

2 How did the animals feel when they found out who Mr. C was? Why?

3 What would you do if you got an invitation from Mr. C?

Make a List

Write a list of other foods Mr. C might serve at dinner. Make a dinner menu using your list.

BEEP!
BEEP!

WHOA!

How did the egg cross the road?

She scrambled across.

**What are two things you
can never eat for breakfast?**

Lunch and supper

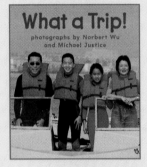

What a Trip!
photographs by Norbert Wu
and Michael Justice

Words to Know

also	some
funny	trap
green	crab
color	grab
like	crack
brown	it's
many	let's
blue	

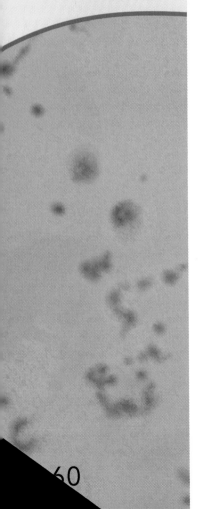

What is in the big wet net?
It's got some big crabs in it.
Many crabs are a blue color.

Lots of crabs are also brown.

Quick! Grab the funny brown crab!

Quick! Quick! Trap the big green crab.

Quick! Let's eat! Get set.

Crack, crack, crack! I like crabs.

Meet the Photographer
Norbert Wu

What a Trip!

photographs by Norbert Wu and Michael Justice

Let's go!
We are going on a fun trip.
We will get wet!

We jump in!
We will be looking in the sea.
What will we find in here?

Here is a funny fish!
Look at its big fins.
It also has big lips for a fish!

We find a big blue fish.
It likes to be in the sea grass.
What is it looking at?

Look! It's a brown crab!
A crab can grab.
Can we get a trap for the crab?

What can the brown crab grab?
The crab can grab a shell. Crack!

Here's a green fish.
It also has blue on it.
This fish looks like it's eating.

Big, big whales live in the sea.
They can eat a lot!
Many whales like to eat krill.

krill

Some fish can change color.

Look! Can you see the fish?

What a fun trick!

Some fish can prick.
Do not grab it!
It's not fun to get pricked.

Many fish zig zag in the rocks.
What funny fish they are!

It's cold in here.
Quick! Let's get back to Mom.

We drip and drip, but we had fun!
What a trip!

Think About the Story

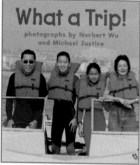

What a Trip!
photographs by Norbert Wu
and Michael Justice

1 How are the fish in the story different?

2 Which fish would you like to learn more about? Why?

3 Would you like to go on a trip like this? Why?

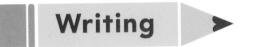
Write a Sentence

Write a sentence about your
favorite part of the story.

I liked
the whale
eating krill.

One, two, three, four, five

One, two, three, four, five,
Once I caught a fish alive.
Six, seven, eight, nine, ten,
Then I let it go again.

Why did you let it go?
Because it bit my finger so.
Which finger did it bite?
This little finger on my right.

Family and Friends

Little pictures
Hang above me.
Pictures of the folks
Who love me.
Mom and Dad
And Uncle Jack,
They love me...
I love them back.

by Arnold Lobel

84

Words to Know

children	picture
come	your
family	dog
father	on
love	lots
mother	plan
people	click

Come look at a picture. It has the people in my family in it.

86

It has my mother and father in it.

It has children in it.

It has six pets in it.

It has my black dog Pal on my lap.

We get lots of love.

Plan to get a big picture of your family.

Who will get in it?

Click, click, click!

Meet the Author
Sheila Kelly

Meet the Author
and Photographer
Shelley Rotner

Who's in a Family?

written by
Sheila Kelly
and Shelley Rotner

photographs by
Shelley Rotner

Who is in a family?
Quick! Come look!
Let's see some family pictures.

Let's snap three pictures.
Click, click, click!
Who is in the pictures?

Click, click!
Look! Sometimes a family is big.
Sometimes it is not big.

Click! Here is a family.
The family has a mother, a father,
and two children.

Mothers can hug.
Fathers can hug, too.
Children can get big hugs.
People can get lots of love in a family.

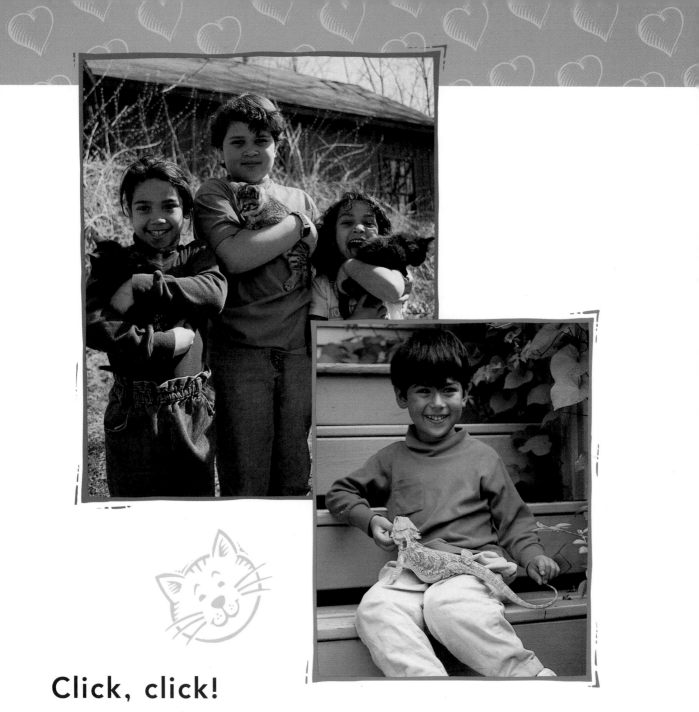

Click, click!
Some families have pets in the pictures.
Look at all the children and pets!

Here is Fluff.
Fluff is a family cat.

Here is Cliff.
Cliff is a family dog.

Click! Here is a family in a garden.
They can dig and pick lots of flowers.

Click! Here is a family that jogs!
They jog on a flat track.
They can jog six laps!

Click! Here is a family on a picnic.
They can get hot food at the grill.

Click! Here is a fun picture.

It is a family tossing a big red ball.

Grab it! Toss it! Do not let it drop!

Here's a plan!
Can you get a picture of your family?

You will be glad to have your family picture.

Think About the Story

 1 How are the families the same?

 2 How are they different?

 3 Does your family do any of the things in the story? What are they?

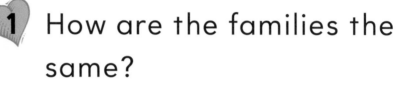

Write a List

Write a list of some things that families like to do together.

Things Families Like
to Do Together

fish

paint

cook

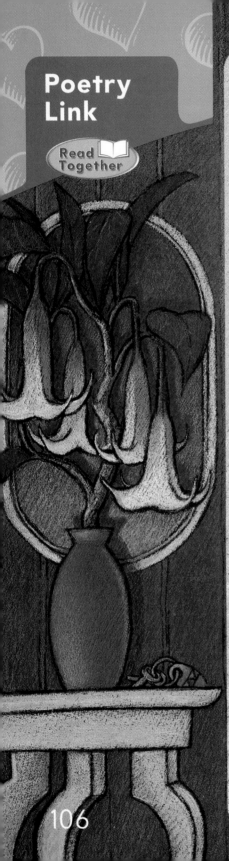

Good Night

Goodnight Mommy
Goodnight Dad

I kiss them as I go

Goodnight Teddy
Goodnight Spot

The moonbeams call me so

I climb the stairs
Go down the hall
And walk into my room

My day of play is ending
But my night of sleep's
 in bloom

by Nikki Giovanni

The Best Pet
written and illustrated
by Anna Rich

Words to Know

friend	best
girl	Peg
know	pet
play	swell
read	ten
she	bells
sing	knock
today	Slim
write	wrist

My best friend is a girl called Peg. She has a pet called Slim Jim.

Read what I write to Peg today.

Does Slim Jim know
a swell trick?

Peg writes back.

Slim Jim can play a swell
trick. He can sit on my
wrist. Slim Jim can sing
and knock on ten bells.

Meet the Author and Illustrator
Anna Rich

The Best Pet

**written and illustrated
by Anna Rich**

My best friend is Peg.
She has a pet bird called Slim.
Slim is a fun pet!

Slim can sing.

Slim can play on big blocks.

We like to see what Slim can do!

One day a sign was at school.

"Look!" I said to Peg. "Let's read it."

"We will write in," I said.

"Slim can get in the Best Pet Test!"

Peg asked, "What can Slim do well?
I know he can sing and play.
Can he win the Best Pet Test?"

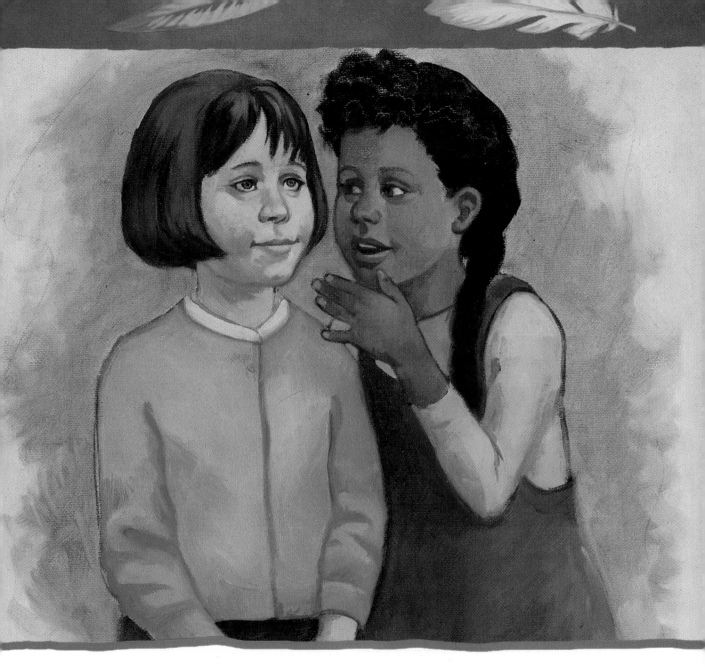

"I know a swell plan," I said.
I tell Peg my plan.
She said, "Let's do it!"

Today is the big day!
Many pets are here for the Best
Pet Test.

One girl had three pet frogs.
The frogs did a trick in a box.
My friends liked the frog trick, but
it was not the best.

One boy had a pet dog who did
a trick on ten bells.
It was a swell trick, but it was
not the best.

Peg and Slim got set.
Everyone looked.
Slim did the best trick of all!

Slim sat on Peg's wrist.
Peg said, "Knock! Knock!"

Slim asked, "Who's there?"

"Ben," said Peg.
"Ben who?" asked Slim.

"Ben knocking on your door
all day," said Peg.

Everyone yelled, "Slim! Slim!"
They all said, "It's the best pet trick!"

Slim got first prize!
Peg and I smiled.
I know Slim smiled, too.

Think About the Story

The Best Pet

written and illustrated by Anna Rich

1 Why do you think the girls entered Slim in the Best Pet Test?

2 Do you think Slim did the best trick? Why?

3 What trick would you teach Slim for the Best Pet Test?

128

Write a Description

Write a sentence about your favorite character or pet from the story.

Moo u.

Knock-knock.
Who's there?
Cows go.
Cows go who?
Cows don't go who,
they go moo.

GRADE A

COWS LIFE

130

Knock-knock.
Who's there?
You.
You who?
Are you calling me?

131

Bud's Day Out

Bud's Day Out
written by G. Brian Karas
illustrated by Clive Scruton

Words to Know

car	their	hug
down	walk	Bud
hear	would	fuss
hold	run	must
hurt	fun	scrub
learn	but	splat

Mom and Dad get in their
big car. I can not hold Bud.
"Walk," I tell Bud. "Do not run."

But Bud can not hear me.
Bud runs down to the car.
Splat! Bud is not hurt.
But I must scrub up.
I fuss. It is not fun.

"Bud, would you learn if you
got a big hug?" I ask.

Meet the Author
G. Brian Karas

Meet the Illustrator
Clive Scruton

Bud's Day Out

written by G. Brian Karas

illustrated by Clive Scruton

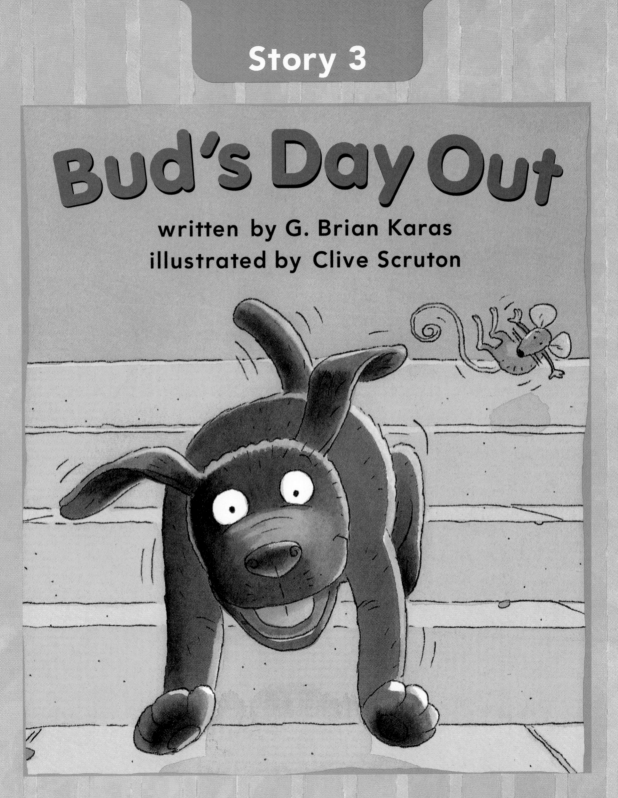

Every day Ben would run in
and hug his dog, Bud.

Bud would run up and down,
but not today.

"Where is Bud, Mom?" asked
Ben. "Is he in back?"
"Let's look for him," said Mom.

138

Ben and Mom did not find Bud.
"Is Bud hurt?" asked Ben.
"Bud is not hurt," said Mom.
"He just got out. Let's go find him."

Ben ran and got in their car.
"Hold on," said Mom. "Let's walk.
Where would Bud go?"

Ben and Mom walked. They met Dan.
Ben asked, "Did you see a big
black dog?"

"Not today," said Dan.
"Why not stop in the glass shop?"

Ben and Mom walked to the glass shop.
"Did you see a big black dog?"
asked Ben.

"Not today," said Jill.
"Why not stop in the pet shop?"

"Did you hear a noise, Mom?"
Ben asked. "I know where Bud is!
Quick! Let's run!"

What a big fuss! Bud and the
animals ran up and down. They
knocked into cans and animal
snacks. Splat! Splat! Splat!

What a big mess!
"Stop! Stop! Stop!" yelled Mr. Plum.
"Hold on to the dog!"

"Come here, Bud!" yelled Ben.
Ben got Bud. Bud got a big hug.
"I am glad to see you!" said Ben.

"Let's scrub up the mess," said Mom.
Mr. Plum felt glad.

Mr. Plum said, "Bud must learn
The Ten Rules for Dogs."
"Gee, what fun!" said Ben.
"I can read, and Bud can look
at the pictures!"

Think About the Story

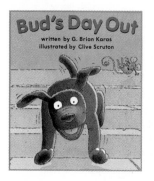

1. How did Ben know where to find Bud?

2. Why did Bud need to learn rules?

3. What would you say to Bud?

Writing

Write a Sentence

Write a rule for Bud.